Spotlight on Reading

Compare and Contrast

Grades 1–2

Frank Schaffer

An imprint of Carson-Dellosa Publishing LLC
Greensboro, North Carolina

Credits

Cover and Interior Design: Van Harris
Development House: The Research Masters

Cover photo © Getty Images

This book has been correlated to state, common core state, national, and Canadian provincial standards. Visit *www.carsondellosa.com* to search for and view its correlations to your standards

Frank Schaffer
An imprint of Carson-Dellosa Publishing LLC
PO Box 35665
Greensboro, NC 27425 USA
www.carsondellosa.com

ISBN 978-16-099-6486-3
04-228137784

About the Book

The activities in *Compare and Contrast* are designed to improve students' reading comprehension skills and to give them the skills necessary for finding similarities and differences in text. With a variety of fun and instructional formats, teachers can provide an introduction, reinforcement, or independent practice for this cornerstone skill.

Use these selections for independent practice or whole-group instruction. Have students work with partners or teams to complete the more challenging activities. Another idea is to place the activity sheets in a center and reproduce the answer key for self-checking.

• •

Table of Contents

Ready for School? 4

School Days.......................................5

Shape Up...6

What Is New? 7

Short, Tall, Big, Small!.......................8

What is Different?...............................9

Match Them Up! 10

Flag Day 11

Two Legs, Four Legs, or Six Legs? 12

City or Country.................................13

Animal Riddles 14

More Animal Riddles 15

Too Hot! Too Cold! 16

What Is the Weather?........................17

Apple Time 18

Line Up! 19

Bug Off!..20

Dogs and Cats.................................21

Big Sharks and Whales 22

What Is the Difference? 24

Diagram Fun.....................................25

Cars and Trucks...............................26

Time to Explore................................28

Snick Snacks 29

Bear Picnics.....................................30

For the Birds 31

For the Birds Again...........................32

In and Out..33

Great Inventions 34

Plant Life 35

Not a Match......................................36

So They Say 37

In the Dog House..............................38

Wheels, Wheels, Wheels! 39

Tortoise or Turtle? 40

Summer Fun 42

Eggs and Ham 43

Good Eye 44

Answer Key 46

Name _____

Look at Tim's back-to-school list. Cut out the things Tim needs. Glue them on the backpack.

• •

**Tim's
back-to-school list**

paper

crayons

glue

scissors

binder

pencil case

pencil

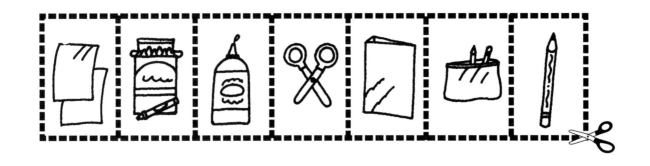

Try this: On another sheet of paper draw a list of your own. Circle things that are on both your list and Tim's list.

School Days

Match the things to the type of school where they would be used. Draw a line from each thing to the correct school.

• •

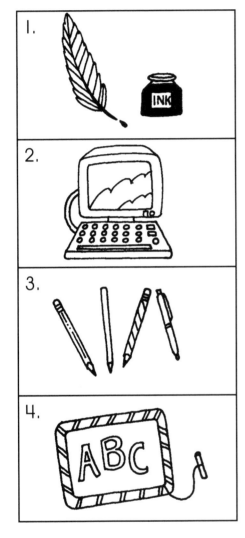

1.

2.

3.

4.

A.

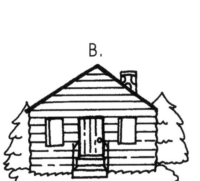

B.

5.

6.

7.

8.

Try this: On a separate piece of paper draw a picture of another thing you use in school today.

Shape Up

Look at the leaves in each row. Color all the leaves that are alike in each row.

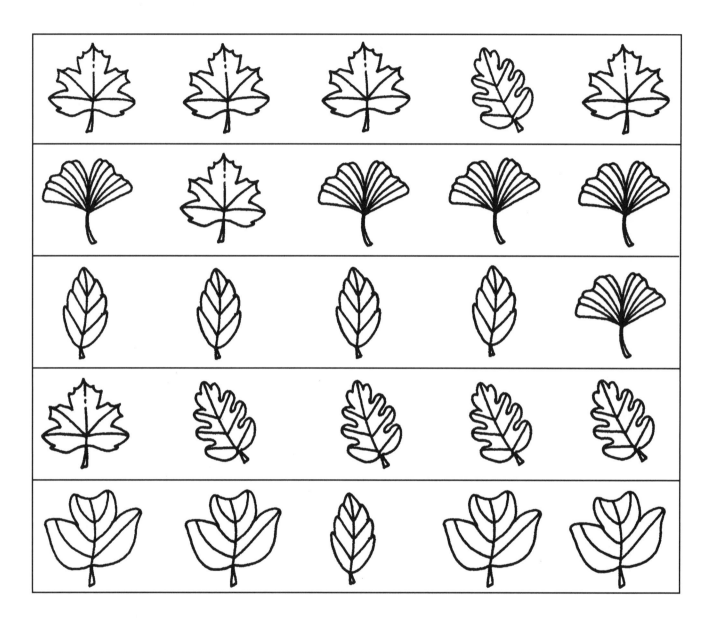

Try this: On a separate piece of paper draw a picture of your favorite tree.

Name _____

Compare the pictures. What has been added to the nest in each picture?
Write the word in the box.

● ●

Word Bank

baby birds   leaves   eggs

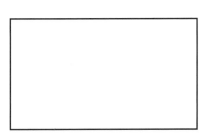

Try this: On a separate piece of paper draw a picture of what
might happen after the last picture.

Short, Tall, Big, Small!

Order the students from the tallest to the shortest. Use the number 5 for the tallest and 1 for the shortest. Circle the correct word in each sentence.

Kate _____ Karen _____ Bob _____ Bill _____ José _____

1. Kate is   taller   shorter   than Bob.

2. Karen is the   tallest   shortest.

3. Bob is   taller   shorter   than Bill.

4. Bill is the   tallest   shortest.

5. José is   taller   shorter   than Karen.

6. Karen is   taller   shorter   than Kate.

Try this: On a separate piece of paper draw a picture of a friend who is taller or shorter than you. Write the name of each person under their picture.

8

Name _____

What Is Different?

Say the four words in each pumpkin. One of the words does not sound the same as the other three. Cross out the word that is different.

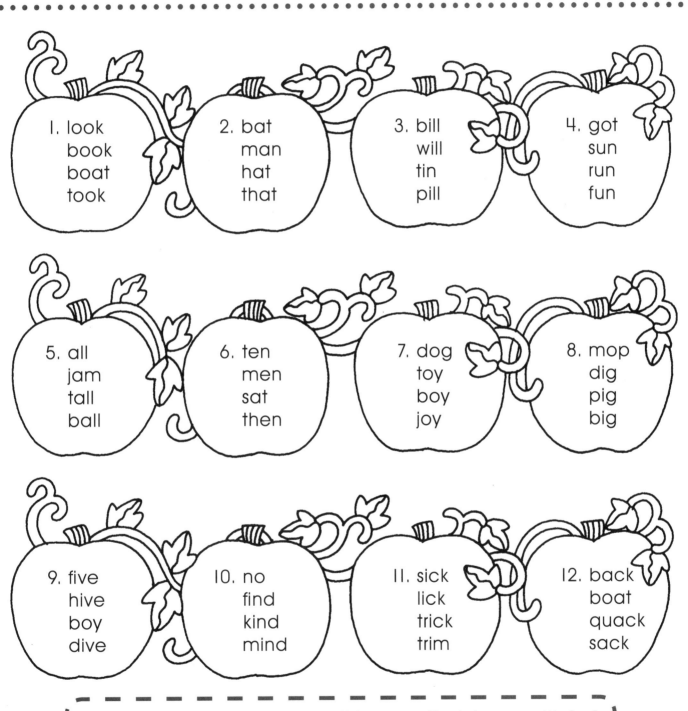

1. look
   book
   boat
   took

2. bat
   man
   hat
   that

3. bill
   will
   tin
   pill

4. got
   sun
   run
   fun

5. all
   jam
   tall
   ball

6. ten
   men
   sat
   then

7. dog
   toy
   boy
   joy

8. mop
   dig
   pig
   big

9. five
   hive
   boy
   dive

10. no
    find
    kind
    mind

11. sick
    lick
    trick
    trim

12. back
    boat
    quack
    sack

Try this: Find three words on this page that rhyme with **hat**. Circle them.

Name _____

 Match Them Up!

Circle the shape that is different in each row.

● ●

A.

B.

C.

Try this: On a separate piece of paper draw another shape that has a circle, a square, and a triangle.

Compare and Contrast • CD-104543

Name _____

Color the flags. Circle the correct answer to the questions below.

• •

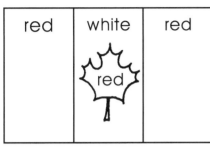

Canada

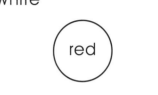

Japan

The Netherlands

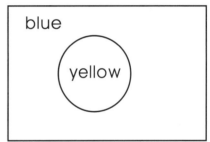

Palau

1. Look at the two red and white flags. What shape is on Japan's flag?

2. What shape is on Canada's flag?

3. Look at the two flags with blue parts. Palau's flag has a _____ ◯.

    white   red   yellow

4. The Netherlands' flag has a _____ stripe.

    white   green   yellow

5. Which two flags are only red and white?

    Palau   Canada   Japan

┌─ ─ ─ ─ ─ ─ ─ ─ ─ ─ ─ ─ ─ ─ ─ ─ ─ ─ ─ ┐
| **Try this:** On a separate piece of paper draw |
| your country's flag. |
└ ─ ─ ─ ─ ─ ─ ─ ─ ─ ─ ─ ─ ─ ─ ─ ─ ─ ─ ─ ┘

Two Legs, Four Legs, or Six Legs?

Cut out the pictures at the bottom of the page. Paste each picture in the correct column.

• •

2 Legs	4 Legs	6 Legs

Name _____

Cut out the sentence strips. Paste the sentences in the correct boxes to make two stories.

• •

City   Country

 **Try this:** Fold a paper in half. On the left side, draw two things you might find in the country. On the right side, draw two things you might find in the city.

a. The looks at the .   e. The brings home the .

b. The drives a .   f. The walks into the .

c. The sees a .   g. A rides in a .

d. A feeds the  and  .   h. A reads on the .

Name _____

Riddles give clues to help solve a puzzle. Look for words that give you clues about how these animals are different. Cut out the animal pictures and paste the correct picture and letter in the box with its description. Make a picture of you to place in the box at the bottom of the page. Write your name under your picture.

● ●

1. I can live in the water or on land.	2. I do not have legs, and I cannot fly.	3. I have a mane.
4. I have spots, and I give milk.	5. It looks like I have two black eyes.	6. I have spots and drink milk.
7. I have two legs, and I can fly.	8. I do have 6 legs, and I can fly.	9. Here is a picture of me.

a. butterfly   b. cow   c. raccoon   d. bird   e. frog

f. snake   g. lion   h. cat   i.

Name _____

Read the riddles below. Write the name of the correct animal at the bottom of each riddle.

Word Bank

   lion   giraffe   tiger   bear   seal   monkey

1. I am big and furry, and I live in a cave. I like to sleep all winter long. I also like to eat honey! I am a _____	2. I have shiny black fur. I love to swim and dive in the water. I eat fish. I can even do tricks. I am a _____	3. I have four legs and a very long neck. My long neck helps me eat leaves from tall trees. I have big brown spots. I am a _____
4. I have a mane and tail. I have very large paws. I make a loud noise when I roar. I am a _____	5. I have a tail and stripes. I have big sharp teeth too. I am a _____	6. I can swing from tree to tree. I have a long tail. Give me a banana, and I will do a trick for you! I am a _____

- -
Try this: On a separate piece of paper name two other animals that can do tricks.
- -

Name _____

Circle either **too hot** or **too cold** to complete each sentence.

• •

1. I put on a if I feel   too hot   too cold.

2. I turn on a when it is   too hot   too cold.

3. I swim in the when it is   too hot   too cold.

4. I put on my when I am   too hot   too cold.

5. I drink cold when I am   too hot   too cold.

6. I pull up my when I feel   too hot   too cold.

7. I wear a when it is   too hot   too cold.

8. I sit under a when it is   too hot   too cold.

Try this: On a separate piece of paper draw a picture of what you like to do when it is too hot or too cold.

Name _____

What Is the Weather?

Look at the picture below. Write the best answers for each question.

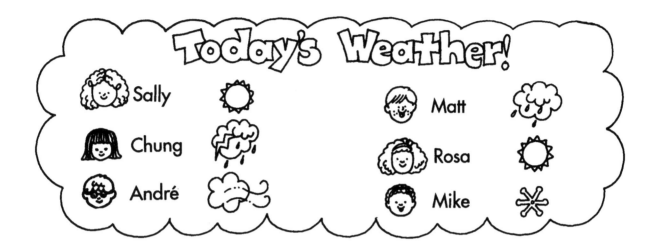

1. Who will have sunny weather? _____

2. Who will have rain? _____

3. Who will have windy weather? _____

4. Which students will need an umbrella today? _____

   _____

5. Who should wear mittens and a hat today? _____

6. Who could fly a kite today? _____

7. Which students may want sunglasses? _____

Try this: On a separate piece of paper draw a picture that shows what your weather is like today.

Name _____

Apple Time

Look at the picture below. Circle the correct answers.

1. Who is holding the basket?

   boy   girl

2. Who is wearing glasses?

   boy   girl

3. Who has a bag?

   boy   girl

4. Who is standing right in front of trees?

   boy   girl

5. Who has curly hair?

   boy   girl

Try this: On a separate piece of paper write how the boy and the girl are the same.

Name _____

Look at the pictures. Draw a **red X** in the boxes under the students who wear glasses. Draw a **green X** in the boxes under the students who have curly hair. Draw a **blue X** in the boxes under students who have freckles. Answer the question at the bottom of the page.

1.	2.	3.	4.	5.
6.	7.	8.	9.	10.
11.	12.	13.	14.	15.
16.	17.	18.	19.	20.

Write a sentence comparing the five children wearing glasses. _____

_____

_____

19

Name _____

Bug Off!

Read the paragraphs about bugs. Read the group of words at the bottom of the page. Draw a line to either the insect or the person to show who has this trait. Circle the traits that belong to both insects and people.

• •

Bugs are insects! They have **skeletons** like you do. But an insect's skeleton is outside its body, not inside like ours.

Insects have three body parts. They have a **head** and a stomach (called an **abdomen**), just like you do. The third part is called a **thorax**. A person does not have a thorax. People do not have **wings**, either. Insects have **wings** to help them fly.

Insects have **legs,** but they do not look like your **legs**! They have **six** legs instead of two. Insects also have **two sets of jaws** to help them chew. They also have **two kinds of eyes**!

A.

1. skeleton
2. skeleton inside
3. skeleton outside
4. head
5. abdomen
6. legs
7. six legs
8. two legs
9. two eyes
10. two kinds of eyes
11. one set of jaws
12. two sets of jaws
13. wings

B.

Try this: On a separate piece of paper draw a picture of a bug you do not like to be around!

Name _____

Dogs and Cats

Read the sentences. If the sentence tells how dogs and cats are the same, circle the word same. If the sentence tells how dogs and cats are different, circle the word different.

1. Dogs and cats are animals.   same   different

2. Dogs bark, and cats meow.   same   different

3. Dogs and cats have four feet.   same   different

4. Baby cats are called kittens,
   while baby dogs are called puppies.   same   different

5. Cats can get up in trees, but dogs cannot.   same   different

6. Dogs and cats can be good pets.   same   different

7. Most dogs and cats have fur.   same   different

8. Cats purr, and dogs do not.   same   different

Try this: On another sheet of paper draw a picture of a cat and dog doing the same thing.

Name _____

Big Sharks and Whales

Read this page. Use the facts you read to complete the chart on the next page comparing whales and sharks.

• •

A giant whale shark is so big it would not fit on a city bus. It is also far heavier than a city bus. The largest tiger shark ever caught was as long as a big car. It weighed more than a big car. A hammerhead shark is shorter than a tiger shark but weighs the same. A tiger shark can weigh about a ton.

The largest sperm whale measured was longer than a big (18 wheel) truck. It weighed almost two times as much as the big truck. The largest humpback whale measured was shorter than a sperm whale. It weighed almost as much as the huge sperm whale. The great blue whales can weigh almost as much as a train locomotive. A blue whale can be longer than two city buses.

> **Try This:** On another sheet of paper draw your own shark.

Big Sharks and Whales (cont.)

Complete the chart comparing sharks and whales.

	Length Compared To	Weight Compared To
1. whale shark		
2. tiger shark		
3. hammerhead shark		
4. sperm whale		
5. humpback whale		
6. blue whale		

7. Which two sharks weigh around a ton? _____

8. Which is the longest animal in the story? _____

9. How did you find your answer? _____

_____

What Is the Difference?

Read the sentences. If the sentence tells how the sun and the moon are the same, write S on the line. If the sentence tells how the sun and the moon are different, write D on the line.

• •

1. _____ The sun is shaped like a ball, and so is the moon.

2. _____ The sun is made of gas, and the moon is made of rock.

3. _____ The sun is a star, but the moon is not.

4. _____ The sun and the moon seem to move across the sky.

5. _____ The moon goes around Earth, but the sun does not.

6. _____ The sun and the moon are far away.

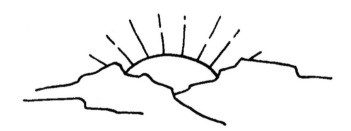

Try this: On a separate piece of paper draw a picture of a beautiful sunrise.

Diagram Fun

In the Venn Diagram, write words from the Word Bank that have the letter r in the r circle. Write, words with the letter t in the t circle. Put words with both r and t in the middle where the circles overlap.

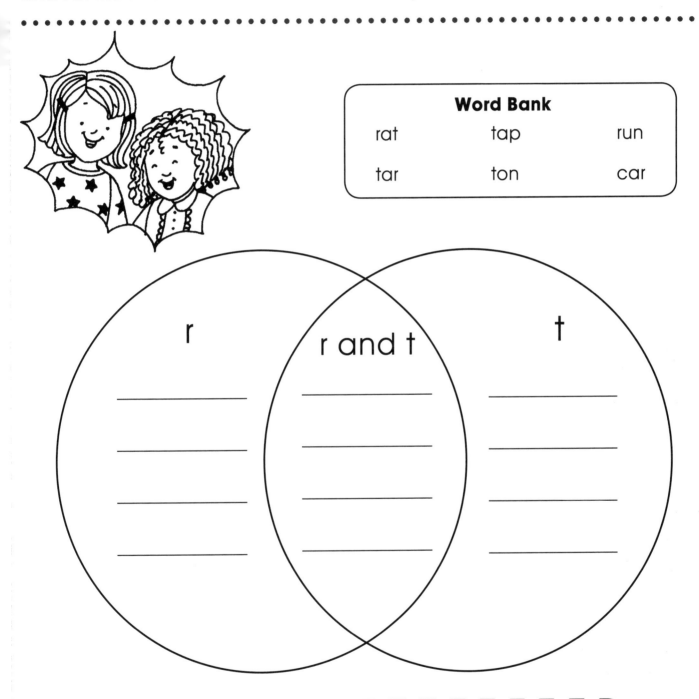

Word Bank

rat	tap	run
tar	ton	car

r

r and t

t

Try this: Think of other words that contain these letters. Write one new word in each section.

Cars and Trucks

Read about cars and trucks. Underline words in each paragraph that tell facts about cars or trucks. Use those words to complete the chart on the next page.

• •

Cars can be fun to drive and have four wheels. Cars use fuel, like gasoline. Cars have trunks to carry things like backpacks and boxes. Cars are made to carry people. Sometimes cars are used by families to go on long trips together. Some cars are used to go really fast. These race cars have room for only one person.

Some people like to drive trucks just because they are big and powerful. Big trucks have 18 wheels. Trucks are often used for work. They carry heavy loads rather than people. They carry heavy loads of cement, wood, and even water. Trucks use lots of fuel to do these jobs.

Name _____

Fill in the chart using facts from the last page. Write words telling about cars in the first column. Write words you underlined about trucks in the third column. Write things that are true of both cars and trucks in the middle column.

Cars	Cars and Trucks	Trucks

Try this: On a separate piece of paper write down three jobs that cars do and three jobs that trucks do.

Time to Explore

Read the following paragraphs. At the bottom of the page circle all the facts about two kinds of explorers.

• •

Long ago, men called explorers sailed across the ocean. They traveled to faraway places. Sometimes they discovered lands like America and Canada. They journeyed to places where sailing ships had never been seen before. They met new people with strange ways. They saw strange birds and plants that did not live in their homelands.

In the 1960s another kind of explorer, called astronauts went to the moon. Astronauts needed powerful rockets to get to the moon. Nobody had ever traveled to the moon before. People on Earth watched on television as the first man stepped out on the moon. Walking on the moon was very easy but getting there was very difficult. The astronauts had to bring their own air and water with them because the moon does not have air or water. Living on the moon would be very strange.

Would you like to be an explorer? You might even travel away from Earth and beyond our own solar system! You might choose to stay here to dive down to the bottom of the ocean. You could even discover a place no one else has ever been before!

What is true about many explorers?

1. Explorers go places nobody has ever been.

2. Explorers like to stay home.

3. Explorers are curious people, like sailors, pilots, and astronauts, traveling to new places.

4. Explorers often find strange new things when they explore.

5. Explorers go places they have already been.

> **Try this:** On a separate piece of paper draw a picture of a place you would like to explore.

Name _____

Maria and Trevor are comparing their snack recipe. Use the recipes to answer the questions.

• •

Maria's Recipe
1/4 cup chocolate chips
1/4 cup raisins
1/2 cup pecans
2 cups cereal puffs
3/4 cups pretzel pieces
1 cup powdered sugar

Trevor's Recipe
1/4 cup chocolate chips
1/2 cup raisins
1/2 cup peanuts
4 cups cereal puffs
2 cups crushed graham crackers
1 cup powdered sugar

Put chocolate chips in a glass bowl. Place in microwave on high for 1 minute. Take out carefully and stir. Stir raisins and nuts into melted chocolate. Stir in cereal and pretzels or crackers. Place powdered sugar in large storage bag. Add coated cereal. Gently shake until mixture is powdery.

1. Which ingredients are the same in both recipes?

    _____

    _____

    _____

    _____

2. Which ingredients does Trevor need that Maria does not need?

    _____

    _____

3. Which ingredients are the same but are not in the same amounts in the

    two recipes? _____

    _____

- -
Try this: On a separate piece of paper make up a recipe
using your favorite ingredients.
- -

Name _____

Bear Picnics

In each box, draw pictures of what the bear likes to eat.

• •

A group of bears planned a picnic. Which bear's picnic basket would sound best to humans. A polar bear? A panda bear? Or a grizzly bear?

Panda bears eat the stems and young shoots of bamboo. Would you like bamboo shoot salad? Pandas also eat birds, snakes, and bamboo rats.

Grizzly bears eat grass, raw fish, ants, wasps, and beetles. Those do not sound very tasty.

Polar bears sometimes eat seaweed and berries. But more often they eat raw fish or seals. In fact, when they are hungry, polar bears will eat anything that cannot get away. It is too cold to picnic with a polar bear. Everything in the basket is probably frozen.

Panda	Grizzly	Polar

Try this: On a separate sheet of paper write the name of the bear that would like to eat grass.

Compare and Contrast • CD-104543

Name _____

Answer the questions at the bottom of the page.

Think About It: If you wanted a bird for a walking partner, which would you choose: a loon, a swift, or a hummingbird?

Answer: None. Loons, swifts, and hummingbirds cannot walk. Although swifts can dive faster than most cars ever move, loons run across the water to start flying. But, a loon can hardly walk on solid ground, and hummingbirds can fly backwards. None of these birds have strong enough legs to support the weight of their bodies. None of these birds would make a good hiking partner.

1. Write a sentence telling how all three of the birds are the same.

_____

_____

2. Write a sentence telling how the hummingbird is different from a loon.

_____

_____

> **Try this:** Which would you like to be, a swift or a hummingbird?
> On another piece of paper write why.

For the Birds Again

Think about the following question and read the paragraphs below it. Underline the sentences that state facts about each bird that help you answer the question. Take a guess and write the bird's name on the line.

• •

Think About It: Which bird can fly longer without landing?

Answer: A sooty tern can stay in the air for years. After it leaves the nest as a youngster, it stays in the air until it is mature—three to ten years. Once in a while it may settle on the water for a short period, but it never lands on the ground. When it becomes an adult, it returns to land to begin a family.

Another long flier is the wandering albatross. The albatross has a huge wingspan, as big as 21 feet (6 meters). It can fly tens of thousands of miles to find food for its young. These trips can keep it in the air for months at a time.

Write a sentence telling how these two birds are the same.

_____

_____

- -
Try this: On a separate piece of paper write something down that would be difficult to do if your feet did not touch the floor.
- -

Name _____

In and Out

Read the story to complete the drawings of In and Out. Label the two animals with the correct names.

• •

There once lived two monkeys. One was named In. One was named Out. In liked to go out. Out liked to stay in. In was all big and black; Out was small and had black and white stripes. One day In went out and did not come back in for along time. Mother Monkey got worried. She told Out to go out and find In.

So Out went out and looked for In. Out found In stuck in a tree. Out went up and helped In down.

When In and Out got home, Mother Monkey asked, "In, where have you been?"

In said, "I was out, stuck up in a tree. But Out came out and helped me get down.

Mother Monkey said, "Good, now Out and In are both in again."

1.

_____

2.

_____

Name _____

Great Inventions

Read the two ads. One of the ads is for something invented a long time ago. The other is an ad for a modern tool. Circle the correct answers to the questions below.

. . . .

The Newest Writing Tool

A personal tool for the 1900s

Handy, little, writing tool that is easy to carry

Ready at a moment's notice

Fits in your pocket or purse

Made of lead sandwiched in wood!

Made and sold by 13-year-old Joe Dixon

Best of all, it only costs 5 cents!

The Everything Tool

The latest, from WizKid, Inc.

So much power, all inside a tiny box!

A monitor, keyboard, and color printer

A great help in all your homework

Set-up is so easy a kindergartner can do it!

All for the reduced price of $999!

1. When was the newest writing tool ad written?

   a. long ago   b. this year

2. When was the everything tool ad written?

   a. long ago   b. this year

3. What is the "newest writing tool"?

   a. computer   b. a pencil

4. What is the "everything tool"?

   a. computer   b. a pencil

5. Which tools do you have at home and at school?

   a. the newest tool   b. everything tool   c. both

Name _____

Plant Life

Read the two definitions. Study the pictures. Then answer the questions.

• •

A **cactus** is from a family of desert plants. They need very little water to grow. These plants have thick main stems, prickly spines, and no leaves. In the spring, they sometimes have flowers. Their roots spread out near the surface to collect rain.

An **oak tree** is a plant with one big main stem or trunk and many branches. Oaks have broad, flat leaves that turn colors in the fall. The seed of an oak tree is the acorn. The roots of an oak grow deep to find ground water for the tree.

1. Write the name of each plant under its picture. **cactus   oak tree**

2. Which plant would grow in the desert?   **cactus   oak tree**

3. Which plant would grow in a forest?   **cactus   oak tree**

_____   _____

4. How are the cactus and the oak tree alike? Circle the phrases below that describe both the cactus and the oak tree.

a. has no leaves   b. has prickly spines   c. has a main stem or trunk

d. needs little water to grow   e. grows branches   f. can have flowers

g. is a plant   h. has broad, flat leaves   i. grows acorns as seeds

j. leaves turn colors   k. has underground roots   l. roots collect water

┌ ─ ┐
Try this: On another piece of paper write a sentence telling
how a cactus and an oak tree are different.
└ ─ ┘

Name _____

Not a Match

Read each statement below. Circle the word groups that do not fit.

• •

1. Boys and girls can eat all these foods:

   a. apples, oranges, pears   b. bowl, spoon, soda can

   c. bread, candy, cereal   d. pudding, carrot, peas

2. These animals do not live in the water:

   a. lion, tiger, bear   b. fish, sea horse, whale

   c. dog, cat, mouse   d. elephant, giraffe, bird

3. These are all big:

   a. mouse, doll house   b. ship, plane

   c. planet, sun   d. mountain, desert

4. These are all small:

   a. baby, puppy   b. raindrop, snowflake

   c. needle, button   d. walrus, elephant

5. These words are in ABC order:

   a. fall, grip, happy, into   b. x-ray, yak, zoo, wagon

   c. push, quack, rush, stay   d. mister, nice, open, play

Try this: On a separate piece of paper make a list of four things that are alike. Write a sentence that tells how they are alike.

Name _____

Read each story. Compare the boldfaced words with the choices below.
Circle the choice that means the same as the **words in bold print.**

• •

Story 1
    Jake always did his work late. He wanted to start doing his work on time.
Jake wanted to **turn over a new leaf.**

    a. Jake wanted to bring a leaf to school.

    b. Jake wanted to do his work on time.

    c, Jake wanted to turn over his paper.

Story 2
    Ann was mad. Her face was red. She would not play with her friends. **She
got up on the wrong side of the bed.**

    a. Ann always sleeps on the same side of the bed.

    b. Ann is not use to sleeping in a different bed.

    c. Ann was in a bad mood.

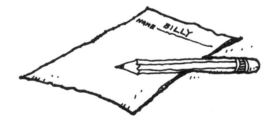

┌───┐
    Try this: On a separate piece of paper
          write another *So They Say* story.
└───┘

In the Dog House

Read each story. Compare the boldfaced words with the choices below. Circle the choice that means the same as the **words in bold print.**

• •

1. Jake did not close the door when he went out. Flies came into the house. Jake **was in a bad place.**

   a. Jake was in trouble.

   b. Jake went somewhere he should not have gone.

   c. Jake was hot.

2. Mike wanted a garden. He did not know what to plant. He asked José to help him. They looked in books. They went to the store together. They chose great plants. **Two heads are better than one.**

   a. Mike has two heads.

   b. Two boys can find out more than one.

   c. José knows more about plants than Mike.

Try this: Do you think the statement "in the stew pot" means the same as "in a bad place" or "two heads are better than one"? Compare and contrast the statements.

Name _____

Wheels, Wheels, Wheels!

Read each story. Circle the letter of the line that completes each sentence below. There may be more than one answer to a question.

• •

Wheels help us do work. They make it easy to move things. If cars, trucks, and trains did not have wheels, they could not move. If your scooter did not have wheels, it would not roll.

A long time ago, men and women carried things on their backs. Donkeys and camels carried things in packs. Sometimes, they dragged things along behind them. It was hard to move things without wheels. Men and women could not move very fast or very far. Donkeys and camels could only carry so much weight.

1. Donkeys

    a. use wheels to move.   b. drag loads.

    c. carry packs.   d. can carry heavy loads rapidly.

2. Trucks

    a. use wheels to move.   b. drag loads.

    c. carry packs.   d. can carry heavy loads rapidly.

3. Scooters

    a. use wheels to move.   b. drag loads.

    c. carry packs.   d. can carry heavy loads rapidly

4. Camels

    a. use wheels to move.   b. drag loads.

    c. carry packs.   d. can carry heavy loads rapidly.

5. It is harder to move things by

    a. using wheels to move.   b. dragging loads.

    c. carrying packs.   d. carrying loads on your back.

Try this: On a separate piece of paper write another way that cars and donkeys are the same and different.

Tortoise or Turtle?

For this science project, use the underlined facts to complete a poster about tortoises and turtles. Write the facts on page 41.

• •

Reptile Fact Sheet

- Tortoises <u>live on land</u> and <u>have front claws for digging</u>.

- Both turtles and tortoises <u>have hard shells</u>.

- Turtles and tortoises both <u>pull their heads into their shells</u>.

- Turtles live in the water and <u>some have semi-webbed feet</u>.

- They both <u>live a long time</u>.

- Turtles and tortoises both <u>lay eggs</u>.

- <u>Some</u> tortoises <u>do not need to drink water</u>.

- There are <u>box turtles and snapping turtles</u>.

Name _____

Fill in the Poster using the underlined phrases from the story.

• •

Turtle   **Tortoise**

1. How is the Turtle is Different

   a. _____

   b. _____

   c. _____

2. How Turtles and Tortoises are Alike

   1. _____

   2. _____

   3. _____

   4. _____

3. How the Tortoise is Different

   a. _____

   b. _____

   c. _____

Try this: Read a book about turtles. Use the list above to
be sure it is a turtle and not a tortoise.

Name _____

Summer Fun

Read the description of each camp. Compare the information given for each camp. Fill in the box with information given in the description. Use the table to help answer Asya's question at the bottom of the page.

● ●

Play Ball Camp

Sign up for six weeks of baseball, basketball, soccer and football. Bring your own game balls and bats. This is an outdoor camp for kids who like to play ball!

Can-Do Camp

For four weeks, turn junk into treasure! In our new building, we will show you how to use junk to make puppets, posters, books, and MORE! Bring your own art supplies.

Weird Science Camp

Sign up for an exciting six weeks outdoors, with experiments, stargazing, and hikes through the woods. All materials provided.

Camp Name	Indoor or Outdoor	Number of weeks	Need to Bring Own Equipment or Supplies
1. Play Ball Camp			
2. Can-Do Camp			
3. Weird Science Camp			

Asya lives in the city and goes to a school that has no sports. She has not been able to use her new soccer ball at all. Asya wants to enjoy the warm summer sun. What camp should she choose? _____

How long will the camp last? _____

Compare and Contrast • CD-104543

Name _____

Eggs and Ham

Write words in the poem that describe only eggs in the area labeled "Egg."
Write words that describe only ham in the area labeled "Ham." Write words
that describe eggs and ham where the circles overlap.

Eggs and ham, eggs and ham,
I like my eggs scrambled around.
Soft and yellow, scrambled around.

Eggs and ham, eggs and ham,
I like my ham fried nice and brown.
Chewy, salty, nice and brown.

Eggs and ham, eggs and ham,
Spoon eggs up and flip ham down.
Spoon eggs up and flip ham down.

Eggs and ham, eggs and ham,
Warm and yummy, swallow them down.
Warm and yummy, swallow them down

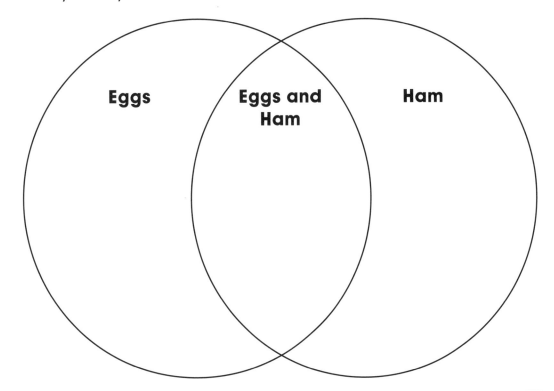

Try this: On a separate piece of paper draw a plate of eggs and ham.

Name _____

Good Eye

Look at the two pictures. Complete the chart.

● ●

Same   **Different**

_____   _____

_____   _____

_____   _____

_____   _____

_____

Compare and Contrast • CD-104543

Name _____

 Good Eye (cont.)

Answer the questions below.

• •

1. Use the information you collected in the chart to write three compare and contrast statements describing the pictures on page 44. Do not look at the picture while you write the statement. Only use the table.

   _____

   _____

   _____

   _____

   _____

   _____

2. Draw a picture of you playing your favorite sport.

3. Write three sentences comparing your favorite sport with a sport you do not like. Underline the things that are alike in the two sports. Circle the things that are different in the two sports. You should have at least two circles and two underlines in your sentences.

   _____

   _____

   _____

   _____

   _____

Answer Key

Page 4
crayons; paper; glue; pencil; binder; pencil case; scissors

Page 5
I. B; 2. A; 3. A; 4. B; 5. A; 6. B; 7. A; 8. B

Page 6
Leaves not colored: leaf 4; leaf 2; leaf 5; leaf I; leaf 3

Page 7
I. leaves; 2. eggs; 3. baby birds

Page 8
3; I; 2; 5; 4
Circle: I. taller; 2. shortest; 3. shorter; 4. tallest; 5. taller; 6. shorter

Page 9
Cross Out: I. boat; 2. man; 3. tin; 4. got; 5. jam; 6. sat; 7. dog; 8. mop; 9. boy; I0. no; II. trim; I2. boat

Page 10
Circle: A. moon; B. tent; C. paintbrush

Page II
Color the flags. Circle: I. circle; 2. leaf; 3. yellow; 4. white; 5. Canada, Japan

Page 12
Two Legs- hen, bird, man; Four Legs- dog; Six Legs- ladybug, ant

Page 13
City- a; f; g; h
Country- b; c; d; e

Page 14
I. e; 2. f; 3. g; 4. b; 5. c; 6. h; 7. d; 8. a; 9. i

Page 15
I. bear; 2. seal; 3. giraffe; 4. lion; 5. tiger; 6. monkey

Page 16
I. too cold; 2. too hot; 3. too hot; 4. too cold; 5. too hot; 6. too cold; 7. too hot; 8. too hot

Page 17
I. Sally, Rosa; 2. Chung, Matt; 3. André; 4. Chung, Matt; 5. Mike; 6. André; 7. Sally, Rosa

Page 18
Circle: I. boy; 2. boy; 3. girl; 4, girl; 5. girl

Page 19
Red X- 3, 6, 10, 13, 18; Green X- 2, 5, 6, 8, 12, 14, 19, 20; Blue X- 6, 12, 17; Sentences may vary but should include the 5 children wearing glasses.

Page 20
A. 3; 7; 10; 12; 13
B. 2; 8; 11
Circle- I; 4; 5; 6; 9

Compare and Contrast • CD-104543

Page 21
Circle: 1. same; 2. different; 3. same; 4. different; 5. different; 6. same; 7. same; 8. different

Page 22–23
Chart Rows: 1. longer than a city bus, more than a city bus; 2. big car, more than big car; 3. shorter than tiger shark, tiger shark; 4. 18 wheel truck, 2 times 18 wheel truck; 5. shorter than sperm whale, sperm whale; 6. 2 city buses, locomotive; 7. hammerhead and tiger shark; 8. blue whale; 9. Answers may vary.

Page 24
1. S; 2. D; 3. D; 4. S; 5. D; 6. S

Page 25
r: rat, run, tar, car; t: rat, tap, tar, ton; r and t: rat, tar

Page 26–27
Answers may vary but should include: Cars-4 wheels, trunks, carry people; Both Cars and Trucks- need fuel, have wheels; Trucks- 18 wheels, used for work, carry heavy loads

Page 28
Circle: 1; 3; 4

Page 29
1. chocolate chips, raisins, cereal puffs, powdered sugar; 2. peanuts, graham crackers; 3. raisins, cereal puffs

Page 30
Answers may vary, but should include: Panda- bamboo shoots, birds, snakes, or rats; Grizzly- grass, ants, wasps, or beetles; Polar- pictures of frozen seaweed, berries, fish, or seals.

Page 31
1. cannot walk, legs not strong; 2. flies backward

Page 32
Underline: Sooty Tern- After it leaves the nest as a youngster, it stays in the air until it is mature- three to ten years. Wandering Albatross- These trips can keep it in the air for months at a time. Answer may vary.

Page 33
1. Out; 2. In

Page 34
1. a; 2. b; 3. b; 4. a; 5. c

Page 35
Write: 1. oak tree, cactus; Circle: 2. cactus; 3. oak tree; 4. c, g, k, l

Page 36
Circle 1. b; 2. b; 3. a; 4. d; 5. b

Page 37
Circle: 1. b; 2. c

Page 38

Circle: 1. a; 2. b

Page 39

1. b, c; 2. a, d; 3. a; 4. b, c; 5. b, c, d

Pages 40–41

1. Only Turtles: live in water, some have semi-webbed feet, box turtles and snapping; 2. Turtles and Tortoises: hard shells, pull heads into shells, lives a long time, lays eggs; 3. Only Tortoises; some do not need to drink water, live on land, use front claws for digging

Page 42

1. outdoor, 6 weeks, own equipment; 2. indoor, 4 weeks, own equipment; 3. outdoor, 6 weeks, equipment provided; questions at end: play ball, camp; 6 weeks

Page 43

Eggs: scrambled, soft, yellow, spoon eggs up; Both: warm and yummy, swallow them down; Ham: fried nice and brown, chewy, salty, flip ham down

Pages 44–45

Chart: Answers will vary but could include: Same- girl's hair, boy's hair, both painting with left hand Different- stripe on boy's shirt, 2 paint brushes in can, boy not wearing glasses, heart on girl's clothes; 1. Answers may vary. 2. Answers may vary. 3. Answers may vary but should have at least 2 items circled and 2 items underlined.

Compare and Contrast • CD-104543